LIFE IS LIKE THE OCEAN

(PART 1)

TALLA BALRAM BALAKRISHNA

Contents

Foreword

Prof K V JAYAKUMAR
Visiting Professor cum Outreach Advisor, IIT Dharwad
Member, Governing Body, Wetlands International South Asia
Former Professor & Dean, NIT Warangal

It gives me great pleasure to write this foreword to a book **"Life is Like the Ocean"**, penned by my student Talla Balram Balakrishna. Right from his student days, I had observed him to be very creative and different compared to others. Over the years, his interest developed from engineering to construction to philosophy culminating in this book.

I enjoyed reading every line of the book, each of the thirteen short stories ending with a lesson from life, starting from childhood to adulthood. The characters he has chosen in the book – Chandramma, Vikramaditya, Achutananda, Balwan, Ramaiah, Prakash, Lakshmi, Venkatesh, and many others – look so realistic and also their lifestyle. The narrative covers various stages in one's life starting from childhood, passing through adolescence towards the adult stage with many unexpected twists and turns, many of the events covered are true to life and one can connect easily to the stories are various stages. Many of the life events can be connected with some aspects or other of the reader.

I congratulate Talla Balram Balakrishna, who has established himself as an engineer cum project manager, who has authored a book on "Construction Methodologies" earlier, and who is well versed with various chapters of Srimad Bhagvadgita, for bringing out the present book. I wish him all the best and all the readers a happy reading.

(K V JAYAKUMAR)

Preface

Dr. Sarbesh Mishra,
Dean and Professor, NICMAR University, Hyderabad.

It is with great pleasure and admiration that I introduce "Life is Like the Ocean" by Mr. Talla Balram Balakrishna. A luminary in the field of project management, Mr. Balakrishna to reach this pinnacle of success navigated through many turbulent waters of the life, working very hard steering them towards success. His insights, motivation & dedication form the bedrock of this invaluable book.

Mr. Balakrishna's life is nothing short of exemplary. His journey, marked by a steadfast commitment to excellence and an unwavering belief in the principles offers readers a treasure trove of wisdom. Born in a below poverty line family he faced many complexities and challenges, his ability to remain calm and composed, much like the ocean in its serene state, has been instrumental in his success.

"Life is Like the Ocean" is not just a memoir; it is a guidebook filled with time-tested principles and learnings that Mr. Balakrishna has meticulously cataloged from his extensive experience. Each chapter reflects his profound understanding of the life and his ability to draw parallels between the vast, unpredictable ocean and the multifaceted realm of passion. Just as the ocean can be both tranquil and tempestuous, so too can the life. It is in navigating these waters that Mr. Balakrishna's wisdom shines brightest.

The pages of this book are adorned with stories of resilience, Patience, and determination. Mr. Balakrishna's experiences serve as a beacon for current and future generations, offering them guidance and inspiration. His ability to distill life's complex challenges into manageable situation is a testament to his efforts & dedication.

What sets this book apart is its blend of real-life experiences and personal reflection. Mr. Balakrishna's narrative is not only about the success he has achieved but also about the personal growth and self-discovery that accompanied his life journey. His stories resonate with the reader, making the principles he shares not only relatable but also actionable.

In a world which continues to evolve and present new challenges, Mr. Balakrishna's wisdom is more relevant than ever. His principles are profound life lessons that remind us of the importance of adaptability, resilience, and foresight.

I invite you to dive into this ocean called life and emerge with a deeper understanding of what it takes to succeed in it.

Happy reading!

Acknowledgements

I want to thank Mr. Chaitanya and Ms. K Dhatri for their invaluable help and support in writing this book. A huge thanks to Talla Bhageerath & Talla Bhagavath for their enduring love and support in everything I do.

My endless gratitude to Sri Prof. K.V Jayakumar Gaaru, **Visiting Professor cum Outreach Advisor, IIT Dharwad; Member, Governing Body, Wetlands International South Asia; Former Professor & Dean, NIT Warangal,** Sri Sarbesh Mishra Gaaru, Dean and Professor, NICMAR University, Hyderabad, Sri. Dr. Venkat Praveen Gannavaram Gaaru, Professor & Head – Srinidhi Institute of Science and Technology for their valuable support & suggestions while making this book.

CHAPTER ONE

DEEP WELL HAPPINESS

You wouldn't be alive if God did not have a purpose for you. It does not matter if you are thirty, fifty, or seventy-five. God still has something for you to do. There are always flowers for those who want to see them.

There was a small village where Chandramma use to stay with her husband Balwan, they had 5 children 2 boys and 3 girls. In that small village they use to earn their living by tailoring, but her husband Balwan was an alcoholic, all the petty income he earned from tailoring he spent on drinking and frequently abused his wife both physically & mentally.

But Chandramma with whatever income she earned from tailoring use to take care of their children and the house, but Balwans brutality had no limits it started growing day by day to such an extent that daily he came to house in intoxicate state and use to hit his wife and even locking them outside their home midnight. Sometimes, Chandramma having no option use to sleep in neighbor's house along with her children.

But Balwan after regaining consciousness use to behave well with wife & children but in alcoholic state, he was a different man, he used to beat his wife ruthlessly without any mercy causing severe trauma to his young children who were just less than 12 years old.

Unable to bear the daily torment, Chandramma left the house one midnight along with her two younger children, her siblings use to stay in nearby village, but she decided not to burden them, with those 2 little younger children, with heavy heart & agony she roamed all night in the outskirts of the village. In completely depressed state of mind, not knowing where to go what to do she stood near to a deep well outside of the village.

She decided to jump into the well along with her children to relieve herself & younger children from her husband's daily abuse, she decided to throw her 4-year-old son first and then tie her 2-year-old daughter to her saree & jump along with her. _All the nature around her the stars, the moon, the trees wanted her to step back, the gods she prayed daily desired she changes her mind. Every entity around prayed for mother's love to win._

She held her son in her hand to throw him in the well, but she was doubtful whether she tied her daughter to her waist properly or not, she kept her son on the ground and started checking the knot she tied her daughter. The boy seeing all these got terrified and started crying uncontrollably, seeing him cry even the dark night, the "well might have cried" but there was no one around to rescue them. Chandramma lifted her son to throw him into the well, but seeing his eyes dwelled with fear & tears Chandramma heart melted, her motherly instincts took over her, she felt what she was doing is sin, she decided to fight in life for her children. Her love towards her children made her change mind. She decided that to fight back in life what we need is patience, she was brave enough to die but she understood that patience is what she need more than the bravery.

The night, the nature happiness had no limit, the well was even more happy as it evaded being witness to three innocent deaths. Mother is happy only when child cries after birth and never again in life she can bear them crying or being sad.

"The strength of a mother is not in her muscles, but in her heart." "A mother's strength is the foundation upon which her family stands." "A mother's strength is the glue that holds a family together in times of trouble."

"Despite all of the suffering in the world, there are also many stories of triumph over it."

"Having kids – the responsibility of rearing good, kind, ethical, responsible human beings – is the biggest job anyone can embark on."

CHAPTER TWO

A FIGHTER WOMAN

Chandramma after escaping death decided to fight back, came back to her home; after seeing her wife back & the ordeal she has gone through Balwan decided to change. They had five children together they named them Vikramaditya, Durga, Lakshmi, Achutananda & Saraswathi.

Chandramma had 2 brothers & 4 sisters; both her brothers had extreme affection towards her sister Chandramma. Chandramma & Balwan in that small village started raising their 5 children doing tailoring, they struggled to make the ends meet and raise & educate their 5 children with the little money they were earning. But Chandramma decided to work even more hard & started searching for other odd jobs, Chandramma was uneducated & Balwan was studied up to 4th class, so she decided to sell clothes in neighborhood villages, she convinced Balwan and started her journey.

Chandramma in the morning use to sell clothes & evening helped Balwan in tailoring works, Chandramma with her hard-earned money started taking care of their children wellbeing but Balwan went again to his old ways spending all his money on drinking. Her Children Vikramaditya and Durga were very good at studies, Vikramaditya studied up to 2nd Grade in their village & 5th grade in other village but nearest high school after 5th grade was 6 kms from where they reside, Vikramaditya use to commute daily 6 kms for his schooling.

But Balwan had other intentions, he decided to stop Vikramaditya from studying any further both Chandramma & Vikramaditya pleaded his father not to do it, but he didn't agree and started teaching tailoring to him ruining his precious childhood.

Child hood trauma can leave you feeling demoralized and damaged. It can make you believe that you are irreparable. But remember that you can always fight the negative forces in your life and restore the peace you once had. If trauma can happen, healing too can happen.

Vikramaditya sacrificed his studies, childhood & started working from the age of 12 years, but Balwan lack of patience and short temper made him beat Vikramaditya mercilessly for even minor mistakes during learning of tailoring, it was such that one day he hit Vikramaditya head to the sewing machine for a minor error he committed while learning.

"Childhood should be carefree, playing in the sun; not living a nightmare in the darkness of the soul."

Seeing her son enduring this daily torture, Chandramma decided to send her son to another place away from Balwan, she pleaded and convinced Balwan to send him to Hyderabad to which finally Balwan agreed, and he dropped Vikramaditya to a relative house & asked them to teach him tailoring. At tender age of 13 Vikramaditya left with no option started working. Chandramma with heavy heart had to send her child away but she was happy within as she was able to save her child from daily misery.

"A mother's sacrifice is a gift that keeps on giving, for it is passed down from generation to generation." "A mother's sacrifice is a silent testament to the depth of her love for her children." "A mother's sacrifice is a reminder of the immense responsibility that comes with being a parent."

"Survivors of abuse show us the strength of their personal spirit every time they smile."

CHAPTER THREE

GOD BLESSINGS

Vikramaditya started living in Hyderabad, even though he didn't have proper food & sleep he worked hard and improved his tailoring skills. Chandramma' s elder daughters Durga & Lakshmi also decided to quit studies from 5th grade after seeing her mother financial struggle and started helping their mother in day-to-day chores.

The youngest son Achutananda starts going to school, Achutananda on other hand loved studies, he was always energetic and jovial child. Achutananda was bright in studies, Achutananda just like Vikramaditya studied up to Grade 2 in their small village, their village dint use to have any school building, daily a government teacher used to teach a group of kids under a Peepal tree. (In the Hindu religion, it is frequently venerated and connected to the trinity Gods Brahma, Vishnu, and Shiva. The tree, which represents life, wealth, and fertility, is thought to be Vishnu's dwelling place. It's usual to see trees decorated with thread, idols, and representations of gods during religious celebrations that honor the peepal tree. The peepal tree is revered by Buddhists as well. Peepal trees, also known as Bodhi trees, are important symbols in Buddhism since it is popularly held that Gautama Buddha gained enlightenment under one. The famous Bodhi tree at Bodh Gaya, Bihar, is revered by pilgrims from all over the world, making it a significant cultural and religious monument.

One of the main benefits of the Peepal tree is that it is one of the most oxygen-producing trees in the world and is known for its ability to purify the air. One mature Peepal tree can produce oxygen for up to 9-10 people in a day. Additionally, Peepal trees can also help in reducing air pollution by absorbing pollutants from the air.

To conclude, Peepal tree holds great spiritual and environmental importance and hence it is referred to as the sacred tree. The Peepal tree is a complete ecosystem in itself and is one of the most important trees in the world).

One day when Achuthananda was in grade 2 teacher asks the children to recite mathematic multiplication 19th table, none of the children was able to do that, but Achutananda recites entire 19th table with ease and confidence, impressed by his skills a Policeman who was standing beside at that moment decides to give him 20 paisa, but Achutananda fears to take the money from Policeman, but his teacher convinces Achutananda to accept the gift. So that 20 paise was the first income Achutananda earned with his skills at the age of 7 years, and he never forgets that in his life.

"Happy times come and go, but the best childhood memories stay forever."

Achutananda completes his 2nd grade in his village, but to study from 3rd grade he must go to neighboring village, Achutananda had 3 best friends, Tagore, Reddy, and Agnathavasi all four of them started attending school in other village happily. All four of them had to go by walk to attend the school, the route was full of snake houses and snakes & also when it rains the route was completely with mud and water but Achutananda love for school & studies made him brave any consequences.

Strength does not come from winning. Your struggles develop your strength. When you go through hardships and decide not to surrender, that is strength.

Among their friends Achutananda was very short & small, all their friends use to call him 'Potti' means short in Telugu. Achutananda friends use to bunk school and play goli & chirragone etc,. all day and return with him to village after school, but Achutananda never skipped school even once for these, Achutananda got worried about their friend's behavior and went to their home & complained about them to their parents, and from that moment Tagore, Reddy, and Agnathavasi never bunked school without Achutananda' s knowledge.

All four of them completed their 5th grade and Achutananda topped in every class, and exams were Achutananda' s favorite time he celebrated them like a festival. Vikramaditya returns home from Hyderabad, he's now an expert tailor but he insists his mother that he need to still improve his skills, then Chandramma decides to send him to Kolkata West Bengal to her sister's place. After Grade 5 Achutananda must move to town as no nearby villages have schools post 5th grade, one of Chandramma' s sisters had no kids, she decided to take Achutananda with her and thus Achutananda starts studying 6th grade at her aunt's home unlike Vikramaditya, Achutananda was lucky enough to continue his studies.

God is not preparing the blessing for you; he is preparing you for the blessing.

Achutananda studies up to 7th grade from her aunt's home, apart from studies Achutananda was very much interested in public speaking, Singing & games. The school in their aunt's village has only classes up to 7th grade to study further till 10th grade Achutananda must go to another village which is 4 Kms far from her aunt's village. Both their aunt and uncle were very happy raising Achutananda as they had no kids, but to spoil the show Balwan enters in Achutananda' s life and asks him to stop studying and learn tailoring, Achutananda heartbeat skipped listening to it.

At the same time Achutananda' s maternal uncle Vishnu's marriage happens, Achutananda takes this opportunity and after marriage, he assembles all their relatives and explains them that he loves studies and it's his life and if he's made to quit studies, he will end his life.

Though you are having many struggles in your childhood but "If you carry your childhood with you, you never become older."

CHAPTER FOUR

GET UP WHEN YOU CANNOT

Achutananda never hated tailoring or consider it as belittle profession because he knows that preserving family heritage & profession is of great value and who ever can master any kind of their cultural skill will be happy all throughout their life. But his love for studies is above everything for him, so he starts convincing his parents saying them that he will do both, he will learn tailoring without discontinuing his studies with much pursuance his parents agree, Achutananda goes back to his aunt and joins in 8th Grade.

Achutananda starts attending school and prior to going to school & after coming back he learns tailoring, mastering various tailoring skills, his love for studies made him to learn these skills fast as he can take out time for studies, so after tailoring chores he used to get back to his books. And Achutananda was not a bookworm whenever he found time after completion his tailoring & studies he used to focus on sports, Cricket was gaining prominence in India at that time, so Achutananda loved playing cricket, apart from cricket he also used to play chess, carroms, Volleyball & Kabaddi and excelled in many of them.

At the time, he had no idea the advantages of playing those games in his spare time, and they had contributed to his development as "A champion is someone who gets up when they can't."

Achutananda childhood friends Tagore, Reddy, and Agnathavasi also continued their studies in other places, they never forgot each other & communicated with each other through post. Whenever there are holidays for school Achutananda use to go to his village & meet his friends and thus their friendship bond grew stronger & stronger. All his three friends were landlords &

rich but they never undermined Achutananda, they enjoyed their childhood playing all kinds of village street games, entire village was in awe of their friendship.

<u>During that period, he was unaware that "friends are the siblings God never gave us."</u>

When he was in Village during holidays, Balwan gets severely annoyed with Achutananda, afraid of his father's anger he runs to his friends Tagore home, Tagore asks him to sleep at his home that day, but Balwan in inebriated state searches for Achutananda with scissors in his hands and reaches Tagore's home, Tagore hides Achutananda in his bedsheet seeing their love for each other Tagore's mother lies to Balwan about Achutananda' s whereabouts. After his father is asleep Tagore drops Achutananda back to his home, Balwan was a different man in when he drinks, in intoxicated state he used to beat his wife & children mercilessly but the next day he used to be very friendly with the family.

Unable to bear the daily torture Chandramma fled from the home, leaving Achutananda & Saraswati with Balwan, Vikramaditya is in Kolkata and his elder sisters Durga & Lakshmi are at their grandmother's home. By the time Achutananda and Saraswati are awake they don't find their mother at home, Balwan is still asleep, worried about his mother he along with his friend Tagore go to search for her leaving Saraswati at home. Achutananda & Tagore desperately starts searching near all the wells in the village thinking his mother has once again decided to commit suicide. All their search goes in vain as they were unable to find Chandramma, Chandramma' s mother & brothers use to stay 4 kms away from her village, Achutananda & Tagore decide to go to their grandmother' s house hoping Chandramma to be there and while waking they search every well throughout the route, but there is no sign of his mother anywhere.

Upon reaching his grandmother's home Achutananda narrates the ordeal to his uncles, listening to it they immediately reach the village with Achutananda & Tagore on cycle. Its sunset time & still there is no sign of Chandramma anywhere. Chandramma hides in the bushes near a well in the village just sitting & unable to muster courage to commit suicide, Achutananda & Tagore searched every well in the village, but they dint go inside the bushes, so they were unable to find her.

Meanwhile a Snake enters the bushes where Chandramma was hiding and sits in front of her, Chandramma on seeing the snake fear runs down her spine, there is nowhere for her to move as the snake was right in front of her, not knowing what to do Chandramma freezes and starts praying to snake, Snake leaves the place without hurting Chandramma, she feels that even god does not want her to die, and at the same time someone from the village passing by notices Chandramma in the bushes, he immediately asks her to come out & drops her at her home.

<u>"Life is not always easy to live, but the opportunity to do so is a blessing beyond comprehension," is something she is unaware of.</u>

Chandramma on reaching home finds her brothers and breaks down, seeing their mother back Achutananda & Saraswati happiness had not limits that was the moment when everything changed, and the fights and disturbances came to an end.

Meanwhile Vikramaditya moves to Dubai with the help of his uncles, and with the monetary help from her son, Chandramma marries both her daughters Durga & Lakshmi. Suddenly Chandramma elder brother Vallabha suffers with a heart attack, as her brother health is deteriorating, they marry Vikramaditya with Vallabha's elder daughter. Everything was going smoothly but tragedy strikes Chandramma again, Balwan due to his heavy drinking habit gets paralyzed and bedridden. Uncertainty looms over Achutananda' s family again.

CHAPTER FIVE

SELF BELIEF & HARDWORK = SUCCESS

As Balwan gets paralyzed, Chandramma appoints a good doctor for his treatment & within few days Balwan starts walking with the support of a stand or walker, Chandramma continues her tailoring works and takes care of the family, Achutananda finishes his 9th grade at her aunt's village & enters 10th grade. Just like he had good friends in his village, Achutananda also made two good friends in his school Ramaiah & Prakash. Achutananda, Ramaiah & Prakash all of them were very good at studies they had healthy competition among them, even teachers use to love them.

"The healthiest competition occurs when average people win by putting above average effort," something that they were unaware of at the time.

All three of their financial status was equal, Prakash's father was blind, so Prakash used to take care of their family along with studies, and Ramaiah's father was a small farmer.

With god's grace Achutananda always had good friends, in their school they dint had a good Math's teacher, so all three of them joined a tuition with a teacher named Gopanna. As Achutananda was very short he used to find difficult to ride a bicycle but anyhow with great difficulty sometimes by walk and sometimes by cycle he used to travel 8 Kms daily to attend the tuition classes.

With 10th grade board exams nearing Achutananda and his friends start studying very hard with great competitiveness, one day when Achutananda was leaving to tuition his uncle asks him to do an important tailoring work and tells him not to go to tuition that day, Achutananda obeys and he comes in and comes out in 10 mins and picks his cycle, seeing that, his uncle gets angry and confronts him why are you going to tuition, I gave you some work, Achutananda replies that he has already completed his work. His uncle gets surprised seeing how quick he was.

Achutananda continues his studies with great zeal and without troubling anyone, Vikramaditya works hard in Dubai and timely sent money to Chandramma and on the other hand Chandramma's youngest daughter Saraswati took care of her paralyzed father just like a baby even doing tough works like bathing him. 10th grade board exams were nearing, Achutananda brain was full of thoughts on what to do after 10th Grade as his family financial status cannot support him for further studies, at the same time Achutananda comes across his school senior who joins Polytechnic after 10th grade. Achutananda starts his research on Polytechnic and finds it as blessing for financially backward students like him and sets a goal to crack Ploytech an exam to enter Polytechnic course.

Achutananda writes his 10th grade exams, and after few days results are out, Achutananda secures school 1st Rank not only school he tops in entire mandal, Achutananda happiness had no boundaries, his hard work has given him fruitful results.

He felt inspired to "believe in yourself and all that you are" following this amazing event. Recognize that you possess a strength that surpasses all challenges. Success is always the result of hard work and self-belief.

Both his school friends Ramaiah and Prakash secure 2nd & 3rd Ranks respectively but his village friends Tagore, Reddy & Agnathavasi fail to clear 10th Grade. Achutananda & Ramaiah study hard for Ploytech and they secure good ranks in them, Prakash decides to become a teacher & starts pursuing Arts.

To join Polytechnic college, Achutananda had to pay a fee of INR 600, his mother Chandramma & Uncle both did not had such hefty sum, not knowing what to do and thinking all his efforts & hard work will go in vain, he writes a letter to his brother Vikramaditya who is in Dubai asking for monetary help, admission day was nearing, Achutananda everyday use to visit post office to enquire whether he received any money order or not, even post man gets annoyed by his daily visits. But one day Achutananda receives a letter from his brother as soon as he opens it, he finds 600 Rupees, his joy had no bounds his face lightens up like a 1000 watts bulb, finally he got the money he was desperately waiting for. Achutananda thanks his brother in heart and takes admission in the college.

God sees your struggle, keep talking to him listen for his direction. God knows when to send exactly what you need.

CHAPTER SIX

EMPTY POCKET NEVER HELD ANYONE BACK

Achuthananda' s Polytechnic admission was in Hyderabad, Achutananda has never been to Hyderabad before, his family is unavailable as his brother is in Dubai, father is unwell and mother is uneducated, So Achutananda request his friend Ramaiah to accompany him to Hyderabad. Ramaiah & Achutananda reach Hyderabad for admission, Achutananda' s mother gives him INR 600 admission fee and some amount which is enough only for his bus fare. Upon reaching to college Achutananda comes to know that Admission process has been postponed to next day due to some strike in Hyderabad and 144 section has been imposed. Both Achutananda and Ramaiah were clueless on what to do, but Ramaiah mustering courage tells to Achutananda that we will spend the night here and complete the admission process and only then get back to village, Achutananda also agrees with him as they both dint have enough money to go back to their village & come back, though Achutananda had few relatives in Hyderabad he dint know their address and as 144 section was imposed all the buses and Autos too were unavailable.

Both stay in the college till evening as Sun fades out, people start coming on to the streets, both then decide to explore Hyderabad by walk, they start from Masab tank then to lakidakapul, Ravindra Bharati, Assembly, Koti and Abids. As its Achutananda' first visit to Hyderabad he notes down names of all the places he is visiting in his Diary. Its night 8.30 PM now, they have idly for night and starts walking towards Tank Bund and in between they find Navarang Movie Theatre and Mahesh Babu' s movie Balachandrudu was running in it, they decide to go to movie so that they can kill some time so by the time movie completes it 12:00 AM in the morning. Both of them watched movie by sitting over the floor (Floor Ticket @ Rs 2/- each).

Still, they have to wait for 6 more hours for admission process to start, they are confused not knowing what to do and where to sleep, with those thoughts in mind they decide to walk towards tank bund. Both Achuthananda & Ramaiah reach tank band and decide to sleep there for the night, time is 1:30 AM now they don't even have blankets to sleep and there were Mosquito's everywhere. They again start walking around tank bund chatting with each other and looking all the Statues on the tank bund road after walking for some time they halt at "Pothanna" Statue and decide to sleep behind the statue, as there were heavy mosquito's everywhere they were unable to sleep but with great difficulty they rest for 2 hours till 4 AM.

Even though there were heavy mosquito's & chilling cold luckily, they won't get sick, maybe they had God's blessings on them, maybe Pothanna wanted Achuthananda to grow successful and recite some of his poems from "Bhagvatham" to everyone. Both now start to walk towards Masab Tank for the admission process, they reach the college and get fresh in college washrooms and wait for the admission process. Achuthananda observes the other students coming one by one for admissions, every one of them is accompanied either by both their parents or their father. Achuthananda gets teary eyed watching that, he misses his parent's presence with him, but consoles himself thinking he had such a good friend like Ramaiah, <u>and he realized that he was unable to alter God's plan.</u>

A college attender comes and asks all the students to get seated in a hall. Admission process begun and Achutananda has done his homework on which course he wanted to opt for. He comes to know that if he picks Civil Engineering there will be many part time job opportunities, so he decides to go for Civil Engineering, and Achutananda name gets announced on mike, Achutananda & Ramaiah immediately go on to the dais. And finally, Achutananda gets seat in Civil Engineering at Nalgonda Polytechnic College and Ramaiah joins Mechanical Engineering course at Masab Tank college. Both were very elated as their life is taking a concrete shape and return to their village happily.

<u>They both held the belief that "it takes sweat, determination, and hard work to make a dream become reality."</u>

<u>With a proud sensation in his heart, Achutananda opens his diary and writes his name there, adding DCE in the brackets.</u>

During admission process students were told that they will be given a monthly stipend of INR 200 during their course tenure, Achutananda is more than happy thinking there be no more financial roadblocks for his studies. After getting back to his village Achutananda shares his joy with his mother Chandramma, and as there is time for classes to start, he decides to go to his uncle Vishnu and resume learning Tailoring. Achutananda has developed good skills in Tailoring, so he feels that his future is secure as he got his traditional skills along with studies.

<u>He knew that "Being interested in a field is the first step towards success in any occupation."</u>

Achutananda reaches Nalgonda and one of his school senior is also studying there, So Achutananda decides to stay in his room as there are no hostel facility in that college, he carries some ration with him and reaches college. Classes start, Achutananda studied in Telugu medium till high school but now the classes were taught in English, Achutananda dint loose hope because of that he had strong belief in himself.

Achutananda had only INR 100 when he lands in Nalgonda after a month he is left with no money, worried he goes to the Principal to enquire about the Stipend, Principal informs that students will start receiving stipend only after 4 months, Achutananda becomes numb listening to that, his mind questions him how is he going to spend 4 months without a single pie in his pocket, uncertainty again looms over him.

He was distressed for money, but he was unaware at that moment that *<u>"Empty pockets never held anyone back. Only empty heads and empty hearts do"</u>*.

CHAPTER SEVEN

NOTHING IS GIVEN TO MAN ON EARTH

Achuthananda having spent his 100 rupees during his first month of his college and the stipend not being sanctioned for the next 3 months is no longer eligible to stay at Nalgonda. This being his condition he returns to his home village and tries convincing his mother Chandramma to arrange him 400 rupees which is just sufficient to pay for his residency at Nalgonda for the next 3 months. His mother who is highly dedicated to educate his son gathers all the money she earns from her little business. Despite a thorough search of the entire house, she could manage only 100 rupees.

Chandramma knowing the money is insufficient for Achuthananda' s needs, still blesses him with the 100 rupees she could manage from the household. Baffled with just 100 rupees Achuthananda starts listing out the expenses at Nalgonda to his mother. He starts of that the room rent alone is 60 rupees and the bus charge for a month is 30 rupees and how would he survive the rest 3 months with just 10 rupees. He bursts out crying for the lack of any other source of money as his brother is in Dubai, father being bed ridden and mother could collect only 100 rupees.

With many unanswered questions of survival at Nalgonda with insufficient money he still decides to leave the village the next morning. _A good education is a foundation for better future, by keeping this in his mind,_ he starts packing all the essentials like rice, pickles, and other requisites. With his mother's blessing Achuthananda leaves for Nalgonda by bus. His journey was very rough with all the thoughts of impossibility to lead a proper college life with just 100 rupees in his pocket for next 3 months.

He sits at a corner seat sobbing over all the questions of life.

He piles up all the confidence and decides to survive the second month and worry about the rest of the months later. Facing these hardships of poverty, <u>he decides to help at least one underprivileged student to attend school in Hyderabad after settling in life.</u>

Finally, he puts an end to these melancholic thoughts and gets prepared to go to college from the next morning. He peacefully survives the first 45 days at college with room rent and bus charges being paid.

Next month's bills having to be paid and being bankrupt once again he loses hope on his education. Neither are his friends close enough to lend money nor his roommate who is a senior is rich enough to pay for him for the next 3 months. Giving up on his education he decides to leave Nalgonda before anyone could notice that he dropped off from his college in lack of money.

Achyuthanada is being crippled by the fact that poverty and failure is overtaking his will to study. To avoid his mother feeling the same about herself for not providing him with enough money for the education he refuses to go back to his village. After thinking for a while, he makes up his mind to earn money from tailoring. His brother-in-law owns a tailoring shop at Bhongir so, he leaves there with all his luggage. He joins there as a worker despite his heart still pulls him to continue college.

<u>He believed that "Nothing is given to man on earth-struggle is built into the nature of life, and conflict is possible-the hero is the man who lets no obstacle prevent him from pursuing the values he has chosen".</u>

CHAPTER EIGHT

LEARNING IS SOMETHING WHICH NO ONE CAN STEAL

As told in the previous chapter Achuthananda leaves to Bhongir to earn money from tailoring. Knowing that his family would endure over the fact that he had quit college due to financial troubles, he hides the truth from them. But his brother-in-law breaks out the news to Chandramma. At that time her second daughter Lakshmi and her husband Venkatesh were at Chandramma' s home. She cries out the entire situation in despair to her daughter and son in law.

Achuthananda and her siblings always shared a great bond and had each other's back in thick and thin. They couldn't abide to the fact that he discontinued his college in lack of funds. Chandramma pleads her son in law Venkatesh with her hands joined to fund Achuthananda with just 400 rupees and that he would get stipend from another 3 months. Venkatesh impressed by the emotional cords that the family holds, couldn't deny Chandramma request and finally makes up his mind to help out Achuthananda with money.

The very next morning Venkatesh leaves to Nalgonda himself with 400 rupees. He consults Achuthananda friends and learnt that he has got a great affinity for education. He brings Achuthananda from Bhongir and hands over the 400 rupees and bless him to be accomplish all his goals and be a victorious man at life. Achuthananda couldn't be more elated to finally meet his friends and being back at his college. He was so thankful to his sister and brother-in-law that he had no words of gratefulness.

"Family isn't always blood. It's the people in your life who want you in theirs; the ones who accept you for who you are. The ones

that would do anything to see you smile and who love you no matter what."

Achuthananda for the next three months studied vigorously without any trouble. Three months later the stipend of 200 rupees per month starts being funded. He is now relieved of all the financial burdens and over the top delighted that no more must lend money for the residency at Nalgonda. Final exams being round the corner he worked even harder. At his school he always used to top the class, but to his surprise he couldn't secure the top rank at college nevertheless managed to pass all the subjects. He blamed his school curriculum being Telugu medium and couldn't cope up with the English at college. Despite he started working even harder from second year.

Achuthananda had shared good bond of friendship with Venu Gopal Reddy and Paparao from first year. Reddy's father was a postman and Paparao's father was a rickshaw puller. Paparao and Achuthananda shared a similar economic background. They always sticked together and studied with a great competitive spirit among themselves. YSK Reddy was another good friend to them and was the first-year topper. He barely used to mingle with anyone and was always into studies. This way Achuthananda and his friends were tagged book worms.

In good influence of friendship Achuthananda never got into any teenage bad habits. He always aced at studies and sports. Working harder he managed to pass out second year in the top 10 list. Yet not satisfied with the rank, he starts putting more time to studies. He beats YSK Reddy and stands at 2nd rank in the final year. Passing out diploma with second rank has brought great joy to Achuthananda and family.

He understood *"The beautiful thing about learning is that no one can take it away from you, even after our death"*- Talla Balram Balakrishna

In his final year his sister Saraswathi gets married to Srisailam. Chandramma and his brother Vikamaditya grandly celebrate the marriage. He even invites his friends Paparao, Venu Gopal Reddy, Ramesh, Ravindrababu and Sleeva Reddy. His younger brother-in-law Srisailam was a tailor. He very well got along with the family and Achuthananda was happy that his sister is married to a great-hearted man. All this brought great bliss to Chandramma family.

Achuthananda at his college had participated in many inter university sports competitions. He was even a tough opponent at competitions like elocution, essay writing and debates. In his holidays he used to give lectures at the government schools in the village and conduct tuitions at home. Spreading knowledge with tuitions he never forced any student to pay fees and accepted it only from the willing. Having the thought of helping a student to tide over the financial crisis he selects two students Ramaraju and Pandu. These two children were always in his special focus and took extra classes from him.

Achuthananda acknowledges that his childhood friend Tagore had failed 3 attempts to 10 class math subjects. With selective chapters and planned strategy, he helps Tagore to prepare for the 4th attempt. He finally cracks the math's subject and passes out with a good score. Another childhood friend Reddy after failing 10 class leaves to Hyderabad without wasting anymore time. There he joins as a casual labor supervisor.

Achuthananda and his friends with a zeal to expand their spectrum of education didn't want to stop with just diploma. They decided to do engineering and to take up an ECET course which is available only at Hyderabad. The money required to do so and the residency charges all together was 3000 rupees. Venu Gopal Reddy gets this amount from his sister and brother-in-law. Paparao earns this money from casual labor. Achuthananda collects the required money from his stipend savings and rest from his mother.

Convincing their families all three of them leave for Hyderabad with their blessings. They rent a small sufficient room in Ramanthapur at Hyderabad. ECET being a tough nut to crack they work vigorously putting their soul and mind into it. The fact that they could afford only government college worked as an extra push on them to work hard. They studied for two months putting 16 to 18 hours in a day. Together they managed to do all the household chores and simultaneously study helping each other. The date for the examination was finally out. All three getting different centers of examination they had to leave to different places on the day of exam.

Wishing one another all the best, they left to their respective centers with great hope. Achuthananda Centre was at Osmania Engg college. Stunned by the colleges great aura he attempted the exam an extra determination to secure a seat in such college. After the exam they returned to their home and eagerly waited for the results. The results were finally out. But Achuthananda village was such remote place that it didn't even receive a newspaper. He had to travel to a town which was 12 kms far way. To get a bus to that village he had to walk 3 kms to the nearest bus stop. With his mother's blessings he leaves to the bus stop.

He gets down the bus at the town and starts flipping through the pages for his number in the results. Acknowledging that he had secured a state rank of 145, Paparao of rank 220 and Reddy of rank 156, he was on cloud 9. On the way back to his village he couldn't hold his horses to unfurl this celebrating news to his family and friends. His kith and kin couldn't be more euphoric on his success and blessed him with a prosperous future.

"If you want to live a happy life, tie it to a goal, not to people or things." Work hard and stay focused to achieve your goals and dreams in life. That is the path to true happiness.

CHAPTER NINE

HAPPINESS IS HELPING OTHERS

As told before Achuthananda and his friends crack the ECET exam with flying colors and three of them are expecting to secure a seat at government colleges. As there was another 2 months for the counselling to start, they decide to join a part time job to meet the expenses at Hyderabad. They didn't want their families to bear the extra burden of their residential expenses and wanted to be independent. So, they leave to Hyderabad in search of part time jobs.

Venu Gopal Reddy stays at his relative's house and finds a part time job nearby. Whereas Achuthananda and Paparao expecting to secure a seat at the Osmania engineering college take a room in the vicinity. As planned three of them got into different part time jobs and starts earning from 2 months prior to the counselling. Achuthananda monthly pay is about 700 rupees.

They were all aware that having a part-time job can give you the extra money you need to live the college lifestyle. If you're on a tight budget, money can be tight for anything from renting a place to eat to buying textbooks. You may avoid worrying about running out of money all the time by taking up a part-time job that gives you some additional cash.

2 months pass by and the counselling had started. Achuthananda and Paparao as expected got into Osmania engineering college and Venu Gopal Reddy secured a seat at JNTU college. Nothing could hold the happiness of the three for everything going as planned.

Achuthananda proudly adds the tag B.E. in CIVIL Engineering to his name. <u>At the time, he believed that the true architect of the 19th century was the civil engineer. The process of planning and supervising the building of tangible structures and systems with the goal of reaching a desired outcome is known as civil engineering.</u>

Later he realizes that he is the first ever man from his village & Mandal to graduate in Govt engineering and is over the top exhilarated that he would keep up not just his family's name but the village name too. His part time job was from morning 9.00 AM to 5.30 PM and his college timings were 6.15PM to 9.30PM. He joined the part time job fixing an agreement with the builder that he would leave work sharp at 5.30 to reach college in time. The builder with no hesitation accepts the agreement but with one condition that in case of any important work he will have to stay back. Achuthananda with no other option accepts the condition as only part time job eradicates all his financial crisis.

With no trouble in the way Achuthananda and Paparao start going to the college and doing their part time jobs simultaneously. As planned before Achuthananda gets done with the part time job and reaches college sharp at 6.15 PM. Ragging was a prevailing act even at the evenings and almost treated like a tradition in engineering college. Soon as Achuthananda enters the college his seniors call him over and give him all weird tasks to perform in colleges public. One of the wacky tasks he was given was to catwalk with a string of leaves and twigs tied around his waist, wrist, and ankle. Despite the task to be performed in the college grounds Achuthananda with no hesitation entertained the seniors with no complaints.

One of the many tasks he got was to reach out to a beautiful woman sitting in the college garden and to collect her details. Achuthananda with no second thought approached her and explained her that he was sent on senior's demand and must collect her biodata. The woman with a smirk gives her details which he carries to the seniors. This way Achuthananda satisfies the seniors demands of supremacy without any disputes and goes to his classes in peace.

To Achuthananda surprise most of the state top rankers in the ECET examination are his classmates. He felt very proud to be a part of this vying atmospheres, YSK Reddy and Paparao being in the same college kind of relieves him from the thought of having to adapt to a new environment and people. Achuthananda and Paparao get done with all the household chores and prepare lunch boxes for themselves and leave to part time job at 8 in the morning. After this they used to go to the college and return home around 10 in the night when they again had to cook for themselves. All this made them very bust the entire day leaving them no time to study.

During diploma Achuthananda used to dedicate most of the after-college hours to study, in contrast he barely could spare some time to study being busy the entire day at part time job and college. He passed diploma in top 2 rank but the condition being different here he just hopes to pass engineering first year in first class. He never wastes a minute that he gets other than college, part time job, and household chores. In diploma he was always a first bench student and listened to every class with great ease and attention. *He believed that one should "live for today, learn from yesterday, and hope for tomorrow."*

But in engineering his college being post his part time job, which is a construction site, he preferred back bench with his clothes untidy and stinking from the sweat and dust at work. Nevertheless, he managed to study and get taken aways by the tiredness from work.

Successfully he completes his first year passing in first class. Together with the 200 rupees stipend and his salary at the part time job he earns 900 rupees per month. This amount was more than enough to meet all his expenses. Most of his classmates came to the college by their own cars. Achuthananda also dreamt of having a car and Kinetic Honda Two-wheeler for which he has to earn a well-paid job after graduating from engineering.

Every holiday and festival were spent at his village with his family. During every visit to his village Achuthananda conducted tuitions to the children and gave lectures at the government schools. He kept the children entertained by conducting little sportive competitions and gifting the winners with chocolates, sweets and other gifts which he bought with his own money. This way all the children in the village were very fond of him and always looked up to Achuthananda being a prosperous man at life.

His students Pandu and Ramaraju on whim he had a special focus on were about to complete their 9th standard. It reminds him of the promise he made himself that he would hold a poor student's hand to tide over any financial crisis. He realizes that's it's time to stand by the promise and decides to take one of them along with him to Hyderabad. He would have the child stay with him in the room they rented and would take over all the financial responsibilities of the child's education. Pandu and Ramaraju both were good students, but Ramaraju was equally sharp and talented at all the subjects. So, he decides to take Ramaraju to Hyderabad.

Before taking the next step he first discusses this with his mother and his best friend Tagore. Obviously, both appreciate him for the decision and encourage him be one of the reasons of another student's success. But the Question that would Ramaraju' s parents accept to send him along with Achuthananda a 20-year-old boy to Hyderabad Left him unsettled. Ramaraju' s father was a toddy seller. Next day Achuthananda and Tagore leave to convince Ramaraju' s father to accept the offer. His father with eyes full of tears accepted the offer in no time and joined his hands as a gesture of gratefulness.

Ramaraju' s parents delightfully bid a goodbye to his son and Achuthananda. The fact that Achuthananda's actions are trusted by the entire village. *It takes nothing to change someone's life—you don't need to be intelligent, wealthy, attractive, or flawless. All you need to do is be concerned.*

"He will be remembered more for your kindness than any level of success you could possibly attain." he did not know at the time.

CHAPTER TEN

LIFE IS HARD FOLLOW YOUR DREAMS ANY WAY!

Achuthananda has decided to help a student financially he takes Ramaraju to Hyderabad on his parents' approval. Ramaraju' s parents couldn't be grateful enough to Achuthananda for taking their son to a city like Hyderabad for education all on his own expenses. Achuthananda joins Ramaraju in a well renowned private school at Uppal for 10th standard. Achuthananda himself was in 2nd year of engineering. He toils hard at part time job after immediately he goes to the college and reaches home tired at 10PM in the night. Ramaraju gets along well with both Achuthananda and Paparao.

Achuthananda and Ramaraju happened to grow strong intimacy rapport togetherness as days passed by. Ramaraju' s absence in the room other than school hours tensed Achuthananda as he feared the fact that he's new to such big a city and would get lost in the crowd. *"Family is the anchor that grounds us, providing a sense of belonging and a support system that extends far beyond biological connections."*

Ramaraju is his responsibility and anything to happen to him Achuthananda life would be at stake. There was no source of communication as none of them had a mobile phone. Ramaraju was active even in sports and immersed in them, few times used to go home late. Out of anxiety Achuthananda used to yell at Ramaraju for being late but he never took it the wrong way.

Achuthananda dream of getting a student out of his financial burdens and providing him with good standard education came true through Ramaraju. Ramaraju being a well poised kid made it easy for Achuthananda to bring him up. This way everything seems to go smoothly.

Just as the shore is calm before a tsunami something bad had happened that derailed Achuthananda from his tracks. It was his father's death.

Achuthananda brother Vikramaditya who is working in Dubai tried hard to return to India for his father's cremation as it's his duty as the eldest son of the family. Despite the tries he fails to return so Achuthananda being the next son takes the responsibility of his father's cremation. Achuthananda realizes that in this depressing incident of the family he is the pillar of strength and tries hard to not shed even a tear. He tells himself that he's emotionally strong and despite people sobbing around him he stays stable doesn't let himself down. But the moment where his aunt approaches his mother Chandramma to break her bangles and wipe off the tilak on her forehead got him shattered. He couldn't help himself but burst out in tears for the scene happening in from of his eyes.

Taking over all the responsibilities of his father's funeral and other ceremonies he completes all of them with a heavy heart. It takes 20 days for Achuthananda to return to his college and part time job. Despite of his absence for these 20 days his builder Venu Gopal Reddy impressed by his sincerity to work pays him the wages of the entire month. Achuthananda feels indebted to the builder for his entire life.

Among all these hardships he manages to complete his 2nd year of engineering in first class. Ramaraju also completes his 10th boards. As believed by Achuthananda he passed 10 grades in distinction. Achuthananda initially brought Ramaraju in the thought of having him in Hyderabad for just one year. But Ramaraju excelling at academics' changes Achuthananda mind. He counsels Ramaraju that Polytech is the right course for economically low-class students like them. Ramaraju instantly agrees and trains himself for Polytech entrance exam.

In his free time Achuthananda took classes and thought Ramaraju strategies to crack the entrance exam. Ramaraju with a great grasping power could learn topics at good speed. He successfully cracks the entrance exam with good rank and gets a seat at Ramanthapur polytechnic college in chemical engineering. Ramaraju and Achuthananda immersed in rhapsodies of triumph breaks out the news to Ramaraju' s parents who felt equally elated.

"Family isn't always blood, it's the people in your life who want you in theirs: the ones who accept you for who you are, the ones who would do anything to see you smile and who love you no matter what."

Achuthananda regularly gets salary hike at his work and receives a stipend of 200 rupees per month. All together he seems to earn 2000 rupees per month in his 3rd year of college. He sends Ramaraju to poly technical college and takes care that he faces no financial crisis. Ramaraju also received a stipend of 200 rupees. They complete their respective years at college. Achuthananda enters 4th year and in no time his final exams also are round the corner. His zeal of taking higher education grows and decides to do MTech. *At least once a day, allow yourself the freedom to dream*.

GATE is the entrance exams for MTech if not cracked he keeps Indian engineering services exam is the other option. GATE is tough but to crack and has an all-India level competition, for in this just few hours of studying wouldn't be sufficient. 90 days was the time of preparation for this exam. For dedicating more time on the exam Achuthananda quits his part time job for three months. His Roommate Paparao also decides to give the same exam. They start going to coaching lessons together and studying for competition. Never reduce your aspirations to match your existing circumstances, 45 days later Achuthananda meets an accident. The bus he was on to his way back home crashes into the road's divider. Achuthananda fractures his left arm and could do nothing but terminate his coaching. His is unable to cook and do his household chores with his fractured hand. So, he decides to go to his one of the sister Lakshmi's home and prepare there for the exam.

Lakshmi's family was a bigger than a joint family. Achuthananda asked his sister for a separate room for preparation and on his request, she manages to give him a room. He dedicates himself entirely to the room and used to come out only during the mealtimes. He begins to prepare for the exam vigorously as he was running short of time. His sister took great care of him providing him with good food and not letting anyone disturb or distract him. Ramaraju on the other hand completes his second year at diploma. Achuthananda successfully attempts the GATE exam and becomes anxious about the results.

"Life is Hard: Follow Your Dreams Anyway"!

CHAPTER ELEVEN

LIFE IS ABOUT UNEXPECTED TWISTS & TURNS

As told in the previous chapter we know that Achuthananda attempts GATE exam and Ramaraju completes his second year in diploma. Now Ramaraju is in third year and his education goes on without any hindrance. In the time of waiting for GATE results, Achuthananda without wasting no time he begins preparing for IES. Keeping his expectations high Achuthananda thought he would secure a seat in one of the IIT colleges. But when the results were out maybe not reaching his expectations, but he was sure as he would be getting admission in NITs.

Admission fee at the NIT college was 13000 rupees even though it was a government college. After joining the college, he will receive a stipend of rupees 2500 per month. With this big amount he is relieved that he'll have no hindrance in his education and that he can take good care of Ramaraju in his needs too.

But first he must pay the 13000 rupees admission fee before joining the college. As he lacks that kind of sum, he decides to loan it from his elder brother-in-law. He pleads his brother-in-law that he would return it in installments every month as he receives a stipend of 2500 rupees. His brother-in-law being a compassionate person lends him the money.

After few months admission process started at NIT Warangal, Achuthananda observes the other students coming one by one for admissions, every one of them is accompanied either by both their parents or their father. Achuthananda gets teary eyed watching that, he misses his parent's presence with him, <u>yet finds solace in the knowledge that he is unable to alter God's plan</u>. He managed to secure a seat in the next most renowned university the NIT Warangal.

"Dream big - even if you don't achieve your ultimate goal, you may still end up achieving something significant along the way"

He was very happy after securing admission in NIT campus at Warangal. His primary school at his village was under a tree and now he has earned a seat in the states most renowned university. Comparing the stage where he came from to the level, he is at now brings great pride and joy to Achuthananda. His roll number at the college was 1 for which he feels much more elated as he always the first roll number at school and missed it ever since for 7 years. The campus was humongous and all the facilities there were up to the mark and felt just like home. His roommate at the dorm was Chandra Shekhar.

His childhood friends at the village were Tagore, Reddy, and Agnathavasi. They shared such strong cords that there was almost nothing that could separate them and each treated others as more than a brother. Agnathavasi gets married and is working at Bangalore, Tagore was pursuing his degree and Reddy works as a supervisor at a small company. On every holiday visit to his village Achuthananda meets the three of them at any cost.

In the next visit to his village when Achuthananda goes to Agnathavasi' s house he realizes that he is on work at Bangalore and only his wife Pavithra was home. Pavithra very well knew Achuthananda as Agnathavasi' s dearest friend and feels joyous on seeing him. As he enters the house, she greets him and gets him a glass of water as a gesture of respect on receiving guests. As she was handing over the glass to Achuthananda she suddenly breaks down choking and coughing out blood which spills over his shirt. Achuthananda' s shirt was all covered in blood and was shocked witnessing what had just happened. Pavithra after getting her senses back and waking up in consciousness she confesses that she has blood cancer.

Pavithra had hidden the truth from Agnathavasi and pleads Achuthananda that she wanted it to remain so. She takes a promise from him that he would never break out the truth to his friend at any cost. But the truth crippled him for his friend rather called brother Agnathavasi must go through such big a hurdle at a very young age. Just the thought of the future of Agnathavasi becomes unbearable for Achuthananda, with eyes full of tears he returns to his college.

Life is not what you expect: it is made up of the most unexpected twists and turns.

M Tech 1st Semester exams date was declared, Achuthananda starts preparing for exams along with his roommate Chandra Sekhar, but even after trying hard he was unable to focus on the studies, his mind is full of thoughts on future of Pavithra & Agnathavasi, & what's going to happen to their life. With great difficulty Achuthananda completes his 1st semester exams, results are out, and he clears it in 1st class, but he doesn't feel any kind of joy or happiness. His heart was full of agony, not knowing with whom to share his distress, Achuthananda cried alone. He was depressed and he started dreaming of those blood stains on his shirt, unable to bear that he decides to commit suicide. *Each of us may think we know exactly what we need to make us happy, what will be good for us, what will ensure we have our happy ending, but life rarely works out in the way we expect, and our happy ending may have all sorts of unexpected twists and turns, be shaped in all sorts of unexpected ways.*

On the other hand, Ramaraju clears Polythenic in 1st class, Achuthananda meets & congratulates him and asks him to pursue engineering & promises him to continue his support, but Ramaraju is reluctant to study any further he don't want to burden anyone anymore even after repeated insistence from Achuthananda, Ramaraju disagrees and joins a job.

Achuthananda was unable to concentrate on studies, studies are the one which he loved the most and he was unable to focus on it, because of it he becomes suicidal, he decides to jump from his hostel building. He tries to repeatedly soothe his mind, but the picture of Agnathavasi & Pavithra continuously flashes before him he is unable to avoid it, as he promised Pavithra, he will not let anyone know about her condition, he suffers alone and decide to die. But Achuthananda has strong grip on Indian epic Ramayana, he remembers life of Hanuman in it, one side his brain was thinking of Ramayana and other side of Suicide.

He remembers how lord Hanuman unable to find Sita thinks of committing suicide, but in the final minute he takes a step back and decides to try one more time and similar way Achuthananda also wanted to give his life one more try & comes back to his room removing all the negative thoughts filled in his mind.

Stories took twists and turns down fairy-tale paths or down very human everyday ones. You think you're at the end of the book, and it's only the end of a chapter.

This way God saved Achuthananda' s life one more time, Achuthananda too decides to take this golden opportunity & gets back to studies.

"Sometimes God takes your life for some crazy twists & turns." _Get up and face it!_

CHAPTER TWELVE

A PERSON CAN CHANGE HIS FUTURE BY MERELY CHANGING HIS ATTITUDE

"Do not lose hope, please believe that there are a thousand beautiful things waiting for you," he reminded himself. Achutananda after deciding not to end his life, musters all the courage in him & gets back to hostel to his roommate Chandrasekhar, he is unable to control his thoughts about Agnathavasi and Pavithra & those blood stains are embedded in his memory. Still 2 semesters are left for him to complete his M Tech in Civil engineering and a duration of 12 months, Achutananda feels that if he concentrates hard on his studies after these 12 months a successful career is awaiting him. Achutananda never enjoyed his college life, Cooking, studies part time jobs he had no time rejoice his student life. In engineering after coming from part time job he used to smell bad due to the sweat because of that Achutananda use to fear sitting on front bench and use to sit on last bench to go unnoticed, he even used to stay away from girl students. But these last 12 months Achutananda decides to balance his life, he decides to enjoy his student life from now on along with concentrating on studies. *The greatest discovery of all time is that a person can change his future by merely changing his attitude. "Whenever something bad happens, keep calm, take a few deep breaths and shift the focus to something positive".the cure for anything is salt water: sweat, tears or the sea.*Total strength of Achutananda' s M tech batch was 13 members, in that that there were 4 beautiful girls Hinduja, Sukanya, Rani & Suhasini. Suhasini was very intelligent girl among them & also semester topper, & also was a great singer, on the other had Hinduja was a brave girl & had very

good communication skills. Both Suhasini & Hinduja stayed in College Hostel, other two girls were very reserved. Excluding girls there were 9 boys in the class including Achutananda. All his classmates were very mature, Achutananda maintained a healthy relation with them. Apart from Chandrasekhar his roommate, Achutananda grew close with another guy name Dhrona.

NIT Warangal campus had a beautiful auditorium and every week college use to project English, Hindi, or Telugu movie every Saturday. 8 of the 13 students use to reside in college hostel & they use to enjoy the movie played every Saturday at Auditorium. Achutananda & Chandrasekhar use to distribute snacks to his classmates during interval in the way by involving with his batchmates Achutananda started to divert his attention from Agnathawasi & Pavithra. NIT Warangal college also use to have a big food court, every Wednesday Chicken joints were served to students, Both Achutananda & Chandrasekhar use to reach food court early every Wednesday as there used to be huge crowd on that day. Reaching early use to tie their hand kerchiefs to the chair to reserve it. And every Saturday there use to be a dry dinner, different kind of fruit juices, Salads & Pastries were served such was the Quality of NIT Warangal food court. There were students from various states across India so weekly 3 to 4 times even North Indian dishes were served to students, among it Achutananda loved Rajma Chawal. **It was wonderful & great campus to stay.**

In that way Achutananda started enjoying his college & hostel life. Occasionally all their classmates even started going to outside Dhabas, Kalinga & Kamadhenu Dhaba were their favorite, they used to celebrate all kind of get togethers there, Achutananda played an important role in organizing these get togethers, Achutananda & his friend Chandrasekhar tasted beer for the first time in this Dhaba's. Both Achutananda & Chandrasekhar loved playing cricket, and every Sunday there used to be cricket matches among the branches, Achutananda being an all-rounder used to bowl the 1st over and was an opening batsman for their team. There were several movie theatres in and around Warangal & Hanumakonda and Achutananda & his friends watched most of the good movies on the 1st day. Thus, Achutananda enjoyed his college life only in the last year of his entire 9 years of college life. _"Life is 10 percent what you make it and 90 percent how you take it."_

Dhrona one of Achutananda' s friend falls in love with his classmate Sukanya and one fine day proposes her but Sukanya rejects his proposal, Dejected Dhrona come to Achutananda for help. Achutananda too tries to convince Sukanya, but she didn't agree, the same Achutananda conveys to his friend Dhrona that she is adamant on her decision, So Dhrona makes up his mind to forget her. Always, Achutananda was ready to do try something for friends when he was not sure on what to do.

2nd Semester ends and Achutananda clears it with distinction. In meanwhile Agnathavasi starts construction of his house in his hometown being away in Bangalore he gives all the house construction responsibility to Achutananda. Achutananda being a loyal friend use to visit his hometown every Saturday and used to monitor the quality & progress of house and gave necessary guidance to the contractor and after few months he successfully completes that project.

In last semester all the students must do an industrial training as a part of Curriculum so for that Achuthananda' s HOD Sri Jayakumar asks Achutananda along with two others Rakesh, Devendra to visit Calicut Kerala for their Industrial training, and meet Dean at Centre for Water Resource Development & Management Institute, Achutananda' s HOD allocates 2 months to carry out their training at CWRDM. All three of them go to Kerala, and after they reach there, they are mesmerized by the beauty of Kerala, the scenic mountains, the lakes, the backwaters they were just left in awe of its beauty, and they reach Calicut watching all the Western Ghats wonders.

After reaching Kerala they could feel that "In every shade of green, Kerala whispers tales of serenity. From the Western Ghats to the Arabian Sea, Kerala is a paradise found".

Three of them were provided with good accommodation in their hostel, in these 2 months they learn many new things, and one of it was to calculate speed of water inside a lake, they do several experiments on it on high level areas above the sea level. They Successfully complete their 2 months training and receive completion certificate after that they head back to their NIT Warangal campus with so many fond memories of Kerala etched in their heart.

And thus, Achutananda complete his last semester with flying colors, and as the last semester ends, various companies start coming to college for Campus placements. Both the Core construction companies & Software companies come to college, but Achutananda is not interested to go for software job, he opts for core job and finally one fine day a Construction Management company comes to campus to select the students. Out of 13students Suhasini & Rakesh already got placed in a Software firm so all the rest 11 students attend the written test and only four of them clear it and Achutananda was one of them the other three were Chandrasekhar, Dhrona & Hinduja. The company asks all the students who qualified the written test to attend the interview in Hyderabad. <u>It was his maiden interview, he spoke to himself</u> <u>*"use all your assets to help you accomplish your goal, hoping to hear good news soon". Don't be nervous you have great potential. All the best!*</u>

CHAPTER THIRTEEN

A NEW JOB IS LIKE A BLANK BOOK AND YOU ARE THE AUTHOR

Achutananda along with Chandrasekhar, Dhrona & Hinduja come to Hyderabad with many dreams in their eyes to attend the interview at Narayanaguda. At one end they were happy but also several thoughts ran in their mind, the company which called them for interview was a good company with great reputation and salary offered was also good, all of them were determined to get this job, and they knew that if they dint get placed in campus, getting job outside is a mammoth task. They all knew as "All their hard work will pay off"

They all were great friends as they spend 18 months together in the same campus they had good bonding with each other, they start discussing the important interview questions among themselves and prepared to give the best shot. In mean time Chandrasekhar name was called for interview, it went on for 30 mins, Chandrasekhar was a jovial guy his face always had smile on it so after the interview Achutananda & others were unable to make out how the interview went, next Hinduja was called inside, her interview also took 30 mins, once Hinduja came out she started explaining about her interview experience but immediately Achutananda name is called and he rushes to the interview room.

Achutananda was confident enough that he is technically strong, he knows his weakness that is average communication skills as he is from Telugu medium background, he was not that confident with his English-speaking skills. Achutananda too completes his interview & comes out, the company asks them to wait for 7 more days for the results. Finally results arrive all four of them gets selected, hearing the news they are elated, and their happiness had no bounds. Offer letters arrive at NIT Warangal campus and they were offered a salary of INR 10000 per month which was very good remuneration at that time. _Success is the sum of small efforts, repeated day-in and day-out_.

Achutananda wants to convey this message to her mother personally and immediately boards a bus to his village with the offer letter in his hand, while travelling several thoughts flash in Achutananda' s mind, he reminds all the incidents which got him to this stage, Policeman offering him 20 paise, His mother almost committing suicide with him in her hands, and how he almost gave up on studies after completing 7th grade due to family pressure & how he stood School & mandal first in 10th grade and the pain he endured while searching for his mother along with his friend Tagore, & after getting seat in Polytechnic for mere INR 600 how he spent sleepless nights thinking about his future and at one stage he had only INR 100 to spend for 2 months and how he cried in a bus for 3 long hours and the pledge he took to succeed, how he wanted to discontinue diploma in between due to lack of funds, but in the same diploma the happiness he felt when he stood 2nd in the final year, & how he got good state rank in engineering common entrance test that goosebump moment, the time when his father got paralyzed when he was in 8th grade and the discouragement he felt at the time, how with his shabby clothes he studied engineering in one of the best colleges of Hyderabad, how he cracked gate exam and entered the NIT Warangal campus, the horrendous situation when his friend Agnathavasi wife suffered from blood cancer & how he decided to end his life overcoming all these challenges how Achutananda secured good job in a good company all these memories flashed in his mind.

After all these 25 years of struggle & happiness, Achutananda went to his mother and told, Mother I got a job in a very good company with a salary of INR 10000 per month, listening to that Chandramma could not believe her ear & asked "Why would they give you INR 10000 per month, what are you going to do?",

Achutananda explains her & makes her believe that he got a very good job, Chandramma gets teary eyed, her happiness had no limits, she shares this news with the villagers & her family.

This way Achutananda struggled for 25 years and focused on the things which are important to succeed in life, he joined the company on January 2001 in Hyderabad, after joining Achutananda & Dhrona were given field & design jobs, Chandrasekhar and Hinduja were allotted Design job. And this way Achutananda completes his student life and enters professional life. _A new job is like a blank book and you are the author._

New job, new life, monthly targets, filed job, office job this way Achutananda runs his professional life happily & successfully.

Success is not final, failure is not fatal, it is the courage to continue that counts. The value of good education has never left Achuthananda. He is not a product of his circumstances. He is a product of his decisions."

The heart of man is very much like the ocean, it has its storms, it has its tides and in its depths, it has its pearls too.

"Life is like the ocean, it goes up and down"! learn to sail along with it

About The Author

TALLA BALRAM BALAKRISHNA, currently the Technical Director and Director of Projects at ACE Ventures Hyderabad, has held many roles in TATA Consulting Engineers Limited for around 14 years, including the completion of TATA's prestigious project "Housing for tsunami-affected people" across the Tamil Nadu seashore during 2005–2006. He worked as a Director and Head of PMO for the Hyderabad region at JLL India Pvt. Ltd. He earned an M.Tech. from NIT Warangal, Telangana, India.

Balakrishna is an alumnus of NIT Warangal and the College of Engineering, Osmania University, Hyderabad. He is the author of multiple books, including "Construction Methodologies and Procedures," which is quite useful for construction, real estate, and civil engineering professionals.

Balakrishna is a motivational speaker; he provides lectures across engineering colleges in Hyderabad and in prestigious institutes like NICAMR Hyderabad and Engineering Staff College of India (ESCI).

Balakrishna is an incorrigible sports lover, and he participated in many sports at the university level. His wife, Sridevi, is an alumnus of Osmania University in Hyderabad. They have two children.

www.ingramcontent.com/pod-product-compliance
Lightning Source LLC
Chambersburg PA
CBHW020513160726
47991CB00007B/2934